Fact Finders®

MILITARY HEROES

BUFFALO SOLDIERS

HEROES OF THE AMERICAN WEST

BY BRYNN BAKER

CAPSTONE PRESS
a capstone imprint

Fact Finders Books are published by Capstone Press,
1710 Roe Crest Drive, North Mankato, Minnesota 56003
www.capstonepub.com

Library of Congress Cataloging-in-Publication Data
Baker, Brynn.
  Buffalo soldiers : heroes of the American West / by Brynn Baker.
      pages cm.—(Fact finders. Military heroes)
  Summary: "Discusses the heroic actions and experiences of the Buffalo Soldiers and the impact they made during times of war or conflict"—Provided by publisher.
  Includes bibliographical references and index.
  ISBN 978-1-4914-4838-0 (library binding)
  ISBN 978-1-4914-4906-6 (paperback)
  ISBN 978-1-4914-4924-0 (eBook PDF)
1. African Americans—West (U.S.)—History—19th century—Juvenile literature. 2. African American soldiers—West (U.S.)—History—19th century—Juvenile literature. 3. United States. Army—African American troops—History—19th century—Juvenile literature. 4. Frontier and pioneer life—West (U.S.)—Juvenile literature. 5. Indians of North America—Wars—1866–1895—Juvenile literature. 6. West (U.S.)—History—19th century—Juvenile literature. I. Title.

  E185.925.B34 2016
  355.0089'96073—dc23

                                2015017097

Editorial Credits
Editor: Jennifer Loomis
Designer: Veronica Scott
Media Researcher: Eric Gohl
Production Specialist: Tori Abraham

Photo Credits
Alamy: North Wind Picture Archives, 14, 15, 17; AP Photo: Eric Gay, 26–27 (bottom); Capstone: 12; Corbis: 9, EPA/Matthew Cavanaugh, 27 (top); Courtesy of Bobb Vann, artist: cover; Getty Images: Stringer/MPI, 16; Granger, NYC: 11, 20; Library of Congress: 4–5, 6, 7, 10, 19, 24, 25 (top & bottom); National Archives and Records Administration: 13, 21; U.S. Army Photo, sculptor Eddie Dixon: 23; Wikimedia: Public Domain, 25 (middle)
Design Elements: Shutterstock

Primary source bibliography
Page 13—"She Fought Nobly: The Story of a Colored Heroine who Served as a Regularly Enlisted Soldier During the Late War" *St. Louis Daily Times* 2 January 1876.
Page 19—Armes, George Augustus. *Ups and Downs of an Army Officer.* Washington, D.C., 1900.
Page 21—Leckie, William H. and Shirley A. Leckie. *The Buffalo Soldiers: A Narrative of the Black Cavalry in the West.* Norman, Okla.: University of Oklahoma Press, 2003.
Page 22—Willard, Tom. *Buffalo Soldiers.* New York: Tom Doherty Associates, LLC, 1996.

Printed in Canada.
032015   008825FRF15

TABLE OF CONTENTS

CHAPTER 1

BLACK SOLDIERS AND THE CIVIL WAR

The Civil War (1861–1865) was the fifth major war the United States participated in since the Revolutionary War (1775–1783). It involved the United States and 11 Southern states. These Southern states **seceded** from the **Union** and formed the Confederate States of America. The **Confederacy** wanted to create its own country to protect its right to own slaves. The Union wanted to keep the United States a single, undivided country. It also wanted to end slavery. This division between the Northern and Southern states resulted in the Civil War.

Beginning in 1861 many free African-American men and runaway slaves tried to **enlist** in the Union army. They wanted to help fight against slavery. None of the men were accepted. At the time laws existed that prevented African-Americans from joining the army.

These laws changed when President Abraham Lincoln issued the Emancipation Proclamation on January 1, 1863. The proclamation freed slaves in areas under Confederate control. It also announced that African-Americans could legally join the Union army. However, the black soldiers were kept in separate units from the white soldiers.

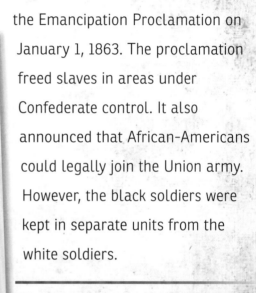

Marriage between slaves was not allowed by law. During the Civil War, African-American Union soldiers, like the man pictured here, were able to legally get married. The war also reunited many black families that had previously been torn apart by slavery. Freed slaves made incredible efforts to find lost loved ones.

secede—to formally withdraw from a group or an organization, often to form another organization

Union—the United States of America; also the Northern states that fought against the Southern states in the Civil War

Confederacy—the Southern states that fought against the Northern states in the Civil War; also called the Confederate States of America

enlist—to voluntarily join a branch of the military

By the time the war ended in 1865, about 186,000 black soldiers had joined the Union army. About 60,000 of them died in battle. More than 640,000 Union soldiers—both black and white—died in the Civil War.

Black soldiers helped the Union win against the Confederate army. Many were recognized for their outstanding volunteer service. A total of 25 black soldiers were awarded with the Medal of Honor for their bravery in the Civil War. This is the highest award in the American military.

The 54th Massachusetts Infantry was a group of black Union soldiers who fought in the Civil War. They became famous after their attack on Fort Wagner in South Carolina on July 18, 1863. Outnumbered by the Confederates, the 54th lost the battle. However, their efforts helped the Union win control of the fort on September 7, 1863. Fort Wagner was just one of many Civil War battles in which black soldiers proved their fearless fighting abilities.

THE 1ST RHODE ISLAND REGIMENT

The Revolutionary War split the American colonists into two groups—the Loyalists and the Patriots. Loyalists were colonists who were loyal to Great Britain during the war. Patriots were people who sided with the colonies. African-American soldiers fought on both sides of the war. Many African-Americans chose sides depending on which army promised them freedom. In 1778 the colony of Rhode Island needed more Patriot soldiers for the war. Colony leaders passed a law that made it legal for African-Americans to enlist. The reward for their service would be freedom from slavery. About 140 African-Americans volunteered and were placed into the 1st Rhode Island **Regiment**. At first the black soldiers were placed into separate units within the regiment. Eventually the entire regiment was **integrated**.

On March 5, 1770, Crispus Attucks, a runaway slave, confronted a group of British soldiers with about 30 other Patriots. The Patriots were unhappy with the British presence in Boston, Massachusetts. Shots were suddenly fired by the soldiers, and Attucks was the first person hit and killed. Although the Revolutionary War was still five years away, many people consider this event, known as the Boston Massacre, to be the first battle of the war. Attucks became the first person killed during the struggle for American independence from Great Britain. Today he is considered a hero by many people.

regiment—a large group of soldiers that fights together as a unit
integrated—accepting of all races

A New Army

|||||||||||||||||||||||||||||||||||||||||||||||

Congress reorganized the army after the Civil War. It voted to allow black soldiers to enlist in the regular army based on their excellent service records. But black men were still not allowed to serve in the same regiments as white men. In 1866 Congress approved the formation of six all-black regiments, both cavalry and infantry. Soldiers who travel and fight on horseback are part of a cavalry. An infantry is a group of soldiers trained to fight and travel on foot. Each regiment had about 1,000 men with white officers as commanders. By 1869 some of the six regiments were combined so that the total number was reduced to four. The all-black regiments now included the 9th and 10th Cavalries and the 24th and 25th Infantries.

Did You Know?

Colonel Edward Hatch was the commander of the 9th Cavalry Regiment for 23 years. Colonel Benjamin Grierson was the commander of the 10th Cavalry Regiment for 22 years. Both men were white.

Western expansion boomed after the Civil War. The U.S. government encouraged American settlers to begin their steady push westward. Rough weather and landscapes made the journey west difficult. Settlers also encountered Native Americans who had already claimed parts of the West as their home. Continuous conflicts erupted among the American Indians, the settlers, and the U.S. government. The black soldiers from the newly formed regiments were badly needed to help with problems that occurred during western expansion.

Black soldiers in service between the 1860s and 1890s were given two uniforms—one for special occasions, such as parades, and one for regular work. These soldiers from the 25th Infantry are dressed for a special occasion in 1883. The first man kneeling on the left is the musician. His uniform, with white braids running across the chest, is slightly different from the others.

CHAPTER 2

BUFFALO SOLDIERS

About 6,000 men joined the all-black regiments between 1866 and 1867. These men would later be known as Buffalo Soldiers, a nickname first given to them by the American Indians. More than half of the recruits had fought in the Civil War. Many of the others were newly freed slaves hoping to escape **discrimination** in the South. The recent end to slavery helped, but blacks were still not treated equally. The laws had changed but the opinions of many white Americans had not. Enslaved people had not been taught to read or write. Most of them could not get homes or jobs once they were freed. **Segregation** continued, and local businesses often would not hire black men.

Infantry soldiers had no horses to help them carry their equipment. Tents and ponchos were rolled up and placed over soldiers' shoulders. Each man also carried a rifle, a backpack, and water. This amounted to 50 pounds (22.7 kilograms) of equipment per soldier. These heavy loads would be carried on foot up to 30 miles (48.3 kilometers) a day in both the burning heat of summer and the freezing cold of winter.

The military offered pay, shelter, education, medical care, and even money during retirement. For many, joining the army was the only way to survive and earn a living. Soldiers ranged from 18 to 34 years old. Most were in their early 20s. Many hoped to prove themselves in the army and gain the respect of white men.

The soldiers had no idea how to survive on the western frontier. However, most committed to at least five years of service. The Buffalo Soldiers were "clothed, armed, drilled, mounted, and sent out on the Plains as fast as they arrived," said one of the **recruits**.

WHY WERE THEY CALLED BUFFALO SOLDIERS?

There are three different stories explaining why the members of black regiments were given the name Buffalo Soldiers.

1. American Indians were known to have great respect for buffalo. The soldiers' dark, woolly hair reminded the American Indians of the buffalo.

2. The soldiers often wore thick coats in the winter that were made out of buffalo skins.

3. American Indians compared the soldiers' fighting to buffalo, both brave and fierce.

Whatever the reason, the soldiers carried the name with honor. The 10th Cavalry Regiment even added a buffalo to the design of its flag.

discrimination—treating people unfairly because of their race, country of birth, or gender
segregation—the practice of keeping groups of people apart, especially based on race
recruit—a new member of the armed forces

CHAPTER 3

THE WESTERN FRONTIER

Beginning in 1867 the Buffalo Soldiers were sent to the western frontier. Part of their job was to protect settlers and keep peace between the settlers and the American Indians. For more than 20 years, the soldiers patrolled Montana, the Dakotas, Oklahoma, Kansas, Colorado, Texas, Arizona, and New Mexico. They served in small, scattered units across huge territories. The Buffalo Soldiers maintained law and order while settlers developed the land. The soldiers were also responsible for building and repairing **forts**, constructing roads, putting up telegraph lines, and guarding food and water sources from enemies.

This map of the western frontier shows the forts where the Buffalo Soldiers served. Fort Davis, located in western Texas, had been used by Union soldiers during the Civil War. It became the headquarters for all four Buffalo Soldier regiments.

A VIOLENT PLACE

The western frontier was a very violent place. Buffalo Soldiers often helped local sheriffs catch criminals. The soldiers chased down robbers and people who stole horses, cattle, and sheep. They traveled alongside settlers, railroad construction workers, and mail carriers to keep them safe. They guarded towns, **homesteads**, **stagecoaches**, and supply routes. The Buffalo Soldiers also guarded American borders and land belonging to American Indians.

AN INDEPENDENT WOMAN

In 1844 Cathay Williams was born into slavery in Missouri. She gained her freedom at the end of the Civil War. As a former slave, Williams could not get a job to support herself. Needing employment, she disguised herself as a man and enlisted in the army under the name William Cathay. She served as a Buffalo Soldier for two years before her secret was discovered. "I wanted to make my own living and not be dependent on relations or friends," she said.

fort—a place built to be strong to keep the people living there safe from attack
homestead—a piece of land with room for a new home and farm
stagecoach—a horse-drawn passenger and mail coach running on a regular schedule with stops

THE STAKED PLAINS

Many Buffalo Soldiers explored and mapped thousands of square miles of unknown territory. The land included thick shrubs, trees, rivers, deserts, and rugged mountain ranges. Temperatures ranged from extremely hot to bitterly cold. Wild animals, such as mountain lions and wolves, were always a threat.

The Buffalo Soldiers' diet included coffee, beans, hard bread and corn bread, beef with molasses, and sweet potatoes.

Fun Fact:

The 9th Cavalry's motto was, "We Can, We Will."
The 10th Cavalry's motto was, "Ready and Forward."

In 1873 more than 400 Buffalo Soldiers were sent to northwestern Texas and northeastern New Mexico. The men traveled for six months through the dry, treeless lands. They battled temperatures above 100 degrees Fahrenheit (38 degrees Celsius) while wearing heavy, wool uniforms. Their job was to explore an unmapped region known as the Staked Plains. The soldiers made maps of the region. They also made sure to write down every water source they discovered. By the time this difficult task was finished, the soldiers had covered more than 10,000 miles (16,000 km) of land. The information they brought back helped settlers plan where to build new towns. The Buffalo Soldiers risked their lives every day to pave the way for future expansion. Eventually roads, schools, churches, and entire towns sprang up around the areas they had mapped.

One of the most important parts of a cavalry soldier's life was his horse. On the frontier it was the horse that got a soldier from one place to another and allowed him to do his job. Soldiers took very good care of their horses because their lives depended on their animals.

A CHALLENGING JOB

It was common for Buffalo Soldiers to be attacked by the people they were trying to protect. Many settlers hated seeing black soldiers wear the blue U.S. Army uniforms. The Buffalo Soldiers were often called names and even shot at by white settlers who did not respect them. This made it hard for the soldiers to do their jobs. Past discrimination followed the men into the army and onto the frontier.

Buffalo Soldiers often protected stagecoaches from robbers wanting to steal the horses and the contents they were pulling. The soldiers became known as guardian angels for the different types of protection they offered throughout the western frontier. They performed this job without complaint despite being treated unfairly by many of the people they were trying to protect.

Some Buffalo Soldiers were assigned to forts in poor condition and packed into filthy housing units. Others battled colds, diarrhea, and lung disease without receiving any medical treatment.

Did You Know?

Criminals who murdered black soldiers were rarely punished for the crime, even if there were witnesses. Instead, black soldiers were often punished if they struck back in self-defense.

Both black and white soldiers were given old or injured horses and used, worn-out equipment left over from the Civil War. Some of this equipment included uniforms, rifles, handguns, **ammunition** belts, saddles, and saddlebags. Food and water were often in short supply. Despite these challenging conditions, the Buffalo Soldiers took their jobs seriously and served with honor.

A cavalry soldier could be no taller than 5 feet, 9 inches (175.3 centimeters) and weigh no more than 155–160 pounds (70–72.6 kg). Horses couldn't carry taller, heavier men plus their equipment. Larger men became infantry soldiers.

ammunition—bullets and other objects that can be fired from weapons

CHAPTER 4

BUFFALO SOLDIERS AND AMERICAN INDIANS

American Indians and settlers often fought over land. The Buffalo Soldiers worked to keep American Indians on their reservations and in return keep settlers off. Reservations are areas of land set aside by the U.S. government for American Indians. This proved to be a tough and dangerous job. White homesteaders, known as boomers, often tried to claim American Indian lands for their own. American Indians would then attack and other settlers were often caught in the middle.

The relationship between the Buffalo Soldiers and the American Indians was unstable. Both groups' goals were at odds with one another. Buffalo Soldiers wanted to be recognized for their hard work and their loyalty to the United States. They also wanted to be recognized as citizens. However, they were working for a racist country. American Indians had many problems of their own. They fought hard to keep their land and their traditions. Buffalo Soldiers and American Indians were both placed in difficult situations and lived challenging lives.

Battle of the Saline River

In 1867 the 10th Cavalry was ordered to find the Cheyenne Indians who killed a group of railroad workers. About 34 men, including 30 Buffalo Soldiers, tracked the Native Americans along the Saline River in Kansas. Suddenly they found themselves surrounded by more than 400 Cheyenne warriors. After eight hours of battle and 2,000 rounds of defensive fire, the men escaped from the Cheyenne Indians. Only one soldier was killed during the battle.

"It is the greatest wonder in the world that my command escaped being massacred," said George Armes, captain of the 10th Cavalry. He credited his officers for "their devotion to duty and coolness under fire." The Cheyenne Indians compared the soldiers to defensive buffalo, both brave and fierce. It was this 100-mile (161-km), two-day patrol that first earned the 10th Cavalry soldiers the respected name Buffalo Soldiers. Later, the name was given to black soldiers in all the regiments.

Along with westward expansion came the building of railroads that ran through American Indian land. The Union Pacific line was built where Plains Indians lived, including the Cheyenne. On August 14, 1867, Cheyenne Indians attacked Union Pacific Railroad workers. The railroad ran through the Cheyenne's homelands and hunting grounds, disrupting their lives.

THE SEARCH FOR VICTORIO

American Indians were not supposed to leave their reservations during the westward expansion of the United States, even to hunt. The U.S. government said they would provide them with food and supplies but failed to keep this promise. Many American Indians were angry, starving, and desperate to find food. In 1879 an Apache leader named Victorio escaped from the Fort Stanton reservation in New Mexico. Victorio was fed up with being forced onto reservations and watching helplessly as his people starved. He raided towns and ranches throughout Texas and New Mexico. He also attacked settlers who stole horses from his tribe and built houses on American Indian land.

The Buffalo Soldiers from all four regiments worked together to remove the settlers and track down Victorio. The soldiers traveled for days on rough mountain trails without food or water, but they never found the Apache leader.

Victorio was born in New Mexico around 1820. After fiercely battling for years to free his people and regain their land, Victorio's brave fight came to an end. In October 1880 he was trapped by a Mexican force in the mountains of northern Mexico where he died.

Although they failed to track down Victorio, the Buffalo Soldiers tried to help the American Indians with problems they faced on the reservations. The soldiers built army forts on reservations to serve as trading posts and as government agencies for many tribes. American Indians often went to the forts to trade goods and get help with issues.

"The work performed by these troops is most arduous. The horses are worn to mere shadows. Men are nearly without boots, shoes, and clothing."

—Colonel Edward Hatch, commander of the 9th Cavalry, describing the conditions during the search for Victorio

arduous—very difficult and requiring a lot of effort

outbreak—when a number of people get sick at the same time from the same germ source

FLIPPER'S DITCH

In 1877 Henry O. Flipper became the first black man to graduate from the U.S. Military Academy at West Point. He was also the first Buffalo Soldier to become an officer. Flipper and other outstanding black officers were never allowed to command the regiments. However, Flipper used his skills in other ways. In 1879 he was stationed at Fort Sills in Oklahoma. Men at the fort were getting sick with malaria caused by mosquitoes. Malaria is a serious disease that people get from mosquito bites. It causes high fever, chills, and sometimes death. The insects were attracted to water that was collecting around the fort. Flipper used his engineering knowledge to design and build a drainage system that removed the water and the mosquitoes. His system ended the malaria **outbreak** and was used by the fort and surrounding community for almost 100 years. The system became a national landmark in 1977 and is still known as "Flipper's Ditch."

CHAPTER 5

HONORING THE BUFFALO SOLDIERS

The Buffalo Soldiers served with courage, discipline, distinction, and honor. They were involved in more than 200 confrontations and battles during the 30 years they were out West. Their brave service on the frontier saved many lives and led to the rapid expansion of settlements. The soldiers paved the way for eight territories to become states and join the Union. The eight states were Colorado, North Dakota, South Dakota, Montana, Utah, Oklahoma, New Mexico, and Arizona. In 1992 a monument was built at Fort Leavenworth, Kansas, to honor the Buffalo Soldiers' service to their country.

"Look at him, Soldier of the Nation—courageous, iron-willed, every bit the soldier that his white brother was. African-Americans had answered the country's every call but had never before received the fame and fortune they deserve. The Buffalo Soldier believed that hatred and bigotry and prejudice could not defeat him, that . . . someday, through his efforts and the efforts of others to follow, future generations would know full freedom."

—General Colin Powell speaking at the dedication of the Buffalo Soldier monument in Fort Leavenworth, Kansas, 1992

The Buffalo Soldier monument in Kansas is 13 feet (4 meters) tall and and is made of bronze. It shows a cavalry soldier riding his horse. The statue was dedicated by General Colin Powell on July 25, 1992. Powell was the first African-American to serve as chairman of the Joint Chiefs of Staff. As chairman, Powell was the senior ranking member of the armed forces and the main military advisor to the president.

bigotry—treating someone of a different religious, racial, or ethnic group with hatred or intolerance

prejudice—hatred or unfair treatment of people who belong to a certain social group, such as a race or religion

MEDALS OF HONOR

Medals of Honor were awarded to a total of 15 Buffalo Soldiers. These medals are given out sparingly. They are awarded to the bravest of the brave who have gone above and beyond the call of duty. The Medal of Honor is a symbol of heroism and is greatly respected.

The Buffalo Soldiers' bravery continued throughout the years. As the original men retired, new soldiers joined the regiments. In 1898 the Buffalo Soldiers were sent to Cuba to fight in the Spanish-American War (April 1898–December 1898) alongside Theodore Roosevelt and the Rough Riders. The soldiers also fought for the United States in World War I (1914–1918), World War II (1941–1945), and the Korean War (1950–1953). The black soldiers helped the United States win many battles and wars throughout history.

In 1889 Buffalo Soldier Isaiah Mays was protecting a U.S. Army wagon carrying gold coins. He and other soldiers were attacked by robbers who stole $29,000 worth of the coins. After being shot in both legs, Mays crawled to a ranch 2 miles (3.2 km) away for help. Mays received a Medal of Honor in February 1890 for his bravery and service as a Buffalo Soldier.

Sergeant John Denny of the 9th Cavalry earned a Medal of Honor for his bravery in New Mexico on September 18, 1879. He helped a wounded soldier to safety while under heavy fire from Apache Indians.

Sergeant Major Edward Lee Baker Jr. of the 10th Cavalry earned a Medal of Honor for his brave actions during the Spanish-American War. He risked his life by facing heavy fire while rescuing a wounded soldier from drowning on July 1, 1898.

Sergeant Henry Johnson of the 9th Cavalry earned a Medal of Honor for his selfless actions in October 1879 in Colorado. He left shelter during an attack from Ute Indians to travel to Milk River. He gathered water from the river and brought it back for wounded soldiers.

In 1948 the U.S. Army integrated the white and black regiments. This was the highest honor of all for the Buffalo Soldiers. White and black soldiers now stand together and fight for America. The Buffalo Soldiers accomplished everything they had hoped to do by enlisting all those years ago.

Fun Fact:

Some Buffalo Soldiers created an organization to remember the history of the regiments. The 9th and 10th Cavalry Association still exists today.

Buffalo Soldiers' bravery, loyalty, and service to their country are still honored today during Veterans Day parades and other ceremonies.

William Dickerson (left) served as a Buffalo Soldier in the 24th Infantry Regiment. On July 23, 2008, he was thanked for his service by Admiral Michael Mullen (right), the 17th chairman of the U.S. Joint Chiefs of Staff. Dickerson was attending a 60th anniversary celebration of the U.S. Army's racial integration.

TIMELINE

1866
Congress approves the formation of all-black regiments in the U.S. Army.

1867
Buffalo Soldiers are sent to the western frontier.

1867
Buffalo Soldiers take part in the Battle of the Saline River.

1873
Buffalo Soldiers explore and map the Staked Plains.

1877
Henry O. Flipper becomes the first black man to graduate from the U.S. Military Academy at West Point and the first black officer in a Buffalo Soldier regiment.

1948
The U.S. Army integrates all fighting units.

1992
A monument honoring the Buffalo Soldiers' service is dedicated at Fort Leavenworth, Kansas.

CRITICAL THINKING USING THE COMMON CORE

1. Why did black men join the army after the Civil War? Use details from the text to support your answer. (Key Ideas and Details)

2. Suppose that Congress never approved the formation of the Buffalo Soldier regiments. How do you think this would have affected the development of the western frontier? (Integration of Knowledge and Ideas)

3. Look at the timeline starting with the formation of the Buffalo Soldier regiments in 1866 and ending with the dedication of the monument honoring the soldiers' service in 1992. What does this say about the effect the Buffalo Soldiers had on the United States? (Craft and Structure)

GLOSSARY

ammunition (am-yuh-NI-shuhn)—bullets and other objects that can be fired from weapons

arduous (AHR-joo-uhs)—very difficult and requiring a lot of effort

bigotry (BI-guh-tree)—treating someone of a different religious, racial, or ethnic group with hatred or intolerance

Confederacy (kuhn-FE-druh-see)—the Southern states that fought against the Northern states in the Civil War; also called the Confederate States of America

discrimination (dis-kri-muh-NAY-shuhn)—treating people unfairly because of their race, country of birth, or gender

enlist (en-LIST)—to voluntarily join a branch of the military

fort (FORT)—a place built to be strong to keep the people living there safe from attack

homestead (HOHM-sted)—a piece of land with room for a new home and farm

integrated (IN-tuh-gray-ted)—accepting of all races

outbreak (OWT-brayk)—when a number of people get sick at the same time from the same germ source

prejudice (PREJ-uh-diss)—hatred or unfair treatment of people who belong to a certain social group, such as a race or religion

recruit (ri-KROOT)—a new member of the armed forces

regiment (REJ-uh-muhnt)—a large group of soldiers that fights together as a unit

secede (si-SEED)—to formally withdraw from a group or an organization, often to form another organization

segregation (seg-ruh-GAY-shuhn)—the practice of keeping groups of people apart, especially based on race

stagecoach (STAYJ-kohch)—a horse-drawn passenger and mail coach running on a regular schedule with stops

Union (YOON-yuhn)—the United States of America; also the Northern states that fought against the Southern states in the Civil War

READ MORE

Honders, Christine. *Buffalo Soldiers.* New York: Gareth Stevens
Publishing, 2015.

Lüsted, Marcia Amidon. *African Americans in the Military.*
Philadelphia: Mason Crest Publishers, 2012.

Orr, Tamra. *The Buffalo Soldiers.* What's So Great About … ?
Hockessin, Del.: Mitchell Lane Publishers, 2010.

Solomon, Sharon K. *Cathy Williams, Buffalo Soldier.* Gretna, La.:
Pelican Publishing, 2010.

INTERNET SITES

FactHound offers a safe, fun way to find Internet sites
related to this book. All of the sites on FactHound have
been researched by our staff.

Here's all you do:
Visit *www.facthound.com*
Type in this code: 9781491448380

Super-cool stuff! Check out projects, games and lots more at
www.capstonekids.com

INDEX